Wolverines

Victoria Blakemore

Table of Contents

What Are Wolverines?

Wolverines are large mammals. They may look like bears, but they are related to weasels and otters.

Wolverines have been given many different names. They are sometimes called skunk bears, gluttons, and carcajous.

Wolverines are usually brown in color. They may have patches of lighter tan or yellow fur.

Size

When fully grown, wolverines are usually around three feet long, including their tail. They are over one foot tall.

Adult wolverines often weigh between fifteen and fifty pounds. Some can be as heavy as seventy pounds.

Male wolverines are usually

larger than female wolverines.

Physical Characteristics

Wolverines have a very thick coat of fur. Their fur helps them to keep warm in the cold weather of their habitats.

Each wolverine has a special pattern of markings on their fur. Their markings are **unique**. No two are exactly the same.

Wolverines have large, **broad**

paws. This allows them to walk

easily through the snow.

Habitat

Wolverines are found in the mountains, forests, and tundra. It is often very cold where wolverines live.

Their habitats are sometimes above the **timberline**. This means that they can live above where the trees grow.

Range

Wolverines are found in parts of North America, Europe, and the Arctic Circle.

They are often seen in
Canada, Alaska, Washington,
and Russia.

Diet

Wolverines are **carnivores**.

They only eat meat.

Their diet is mainly made up of animals such as moose, caribou, squirrels, hares, and porcupines. They have also been known to eat eggs.

Wolverines have a very good sense of smell. They use it to find their prey.

In the winter, wolverines are often **scavengers**. They eat the leftovers from other animals.

They are also able to catch larger animals in the winter. The deep snow makes it easier for them to catch moose and caribou.

Wolverines have very strong teeth and jaws. They are able to eat meat and bones, even when they are frozen.

Communication

Wolverines use mainly sound and scent to communicate with each other and other animals.

They have special scent glands. They **produce** a scent that wolverines can use to mark their **territory**.

Wolverines that are angry may growl and grunt. They will also show their teeth as a warning.

Movement

Wolverines are not usually very fast. They have been known to reach speeds of up to thirty miles per hour, but this is rare.

Since they aren't very fast, they do not usually chase their prey. They prefer to hide and wait to pounce.

Wolverines are very good at climbing. Their sharp claws help them to climb trees.

Wolverine Kits

Wolverines have a **litter** of up to five babies. Their babies are called kits.

Kits are born in dens that mother wolverines dig into the snow and dirt. The dens help to keep the kits warm and safe from larger predators.

Wolverine kits are born white in
color. Their fur darkens as they
get older.

Wolverine Life

Wolverines are usually **solitary** animals. They spend most of their time alone.

Although wolverines are able to climb trees, they are most often found on the ground. They are also able to swim to cross rivers.

Wolverines are active during the day and at night. They do not **hibernate** in the winter.

Predators

Adult wolverines are safe from most predators. They are able to **defend** themselves from bears, wolves, and mountain lions.

Young wolverines are more likely to be prey for larger animals.

Wolverines are **apex predators** in their habitats. They are at the top of the food chain.

Population

As a whole, wolverines are not **endangered**. There are many in the wild. However, in certain places, they are **endangered**. There are not many left in the wild in those areas.

The population of wolverines is **declining** in most areas.

In the wild, wolverines often live

between five and thirteen

years.

Wolverines in Danger

Wolverines are facing several threats from humans. Their habitats are being destroyed by logging and rising temperatures.

In some places, wolverines are hunted for their fur. They are also killed to prevent them from eating **livestock**.

Wolverine habitats are smaller

and more spread out. This makes

it hard for them to survive.

Helping Wolverines

Special protected areas have been set up to provide animals like wolverines with safe habitats. They keep wolverines safe from hunting and trapping.

In some countries, there are **restrictions** on when wolverines can be hunted and how many can be caught.

Researchers are studying wolverines. They hope that learning more about wolverines will allow us to help them.

There are also groups that are working to protect **livestock** from wolverines. They are trying to prevent **conflict** between wolverines and people.

Glossary

Apex predator: the top predator

Broad: wide

Carnivore: an animal that eats only meat

Conflict: fight or disagreement

Declining: getting smaller

Defend: to protect

Endangered: at risk of becoming extinct

Hibernate: when animals sleep through the winter because less food is available

Litter: a group of animals born at the same time

Livestock: animals such as sheep and cows that are kept by people

Produce: to make

Restriction: something that limits or prevents

Scavengers: animals that eat dead animals or plants

Solitary: living alone

Territory: an area of land that an animal clams as its own

Timberline: the land above which no trees will grow

Unique: one of a kind, special

About the Author

Victoria Blakemore is a first grade

teacher in Southwest Florida with a

passion for reading.

You can visit her at

www.elementaryexplorers.com

Also in This Series

Gray Wolves	Sloths	Flamingos	Camels	Koalas	Honey Bees	Pandas
Pangolins	White-Tailed Deer	Orcas	Giraffes	Corn	Meerkats	Echidnas
Walruses	Raccoons	Bald Eagles	Apples	Arctic Foxes	Red Pandas	Cassowaries
Tigers	Ladybugs	Moose	Beluga Whales	Leopards	Elephants	Jellyfish
Binturongs	Lions	Dolphins	Reindeer	Hammerhead Sharks	Hippos	Pumpkins
Peafowl	Chameleons	Florida Panthers	Aye-Ayes	Black Bears	Cheetahs	Manatees
Gingerbread	Polar Bears	Hot Chocolate	Orangutans	Coyotes	Marshmallows	Strawberries

Also in This Series

Aardvarks	**Mako Sharks**	**Alligators**	**Frogs**	**Hedgehogs**	**Brown Bears**	**Bongos**
Sea Turtles	**Quokkas**	**Muskrats**	**Zebras**	**Red Foxes**	**Ring-Tailed Lemurs**	**Platypuses**
Anteaters	**Kangaroos**	**Rhinos**	**Jaguars**	**Wombats**	**Capybaras**	**Gorillas**
Cats	**Skunks**	**Butterflies**	**Dingoes**	**Snow Leopards**	**African Wild Dogs**	**Penguins**
Whale Sharks	**Wolverines**	**Warthogs**	**Caracals**			

Victoria Blakemore